NOTHING BEATS A FAILURE BUT A TRY

A MEMOIR

About

My Three Husbands

KIMBERLY M. ROSS

NOTHING BEATS A FAILURE BUT A TRY!

A Memoir About My Three Husbands

KIMBERLY M. ROSS

For information regarding special discounts for bulk purchases or services, or to simply, speak with the author contact: kimross6615@yahoo.com

ISBN: 978-1-4583-9155

My Dedication and Inspiration

I would sincerely like to thank my mommy for being my best friend and inspirational confidant. Mom, you are a strong, smart, confident, beautiful, black woman and single parent who raised four beautiful children all alone for over 15 years. You managed to retire from Corrections by the age of 57, which is a tremendous achievement. You also had the blessing of purchasing two homes in your lifetime. Do not let anyone tell you that you are less worthy than you are because if it were not for you, we would not be the well-respected individuals we are today. You have always been an inspiration to all of us, encouraging us to be the best we can be. I know that I have gone through some unnecessary changes that I really did not have to go through if only I had listened to you. However, I learned valuable lessons. When we are young, we think we know everything. Now I see how I could have avoided so many trials by just listening. In addition, I see now how difficult it is to raise daughters, but we have a strong foundation and I know, with God's Grace, they will be just fine!

ACKNOWLEDGEMENTS

I would like to acknowledge God, who has always been my strength, my keeper, and my guide. Without Him, I would not be here today. I also give special thanks to my husband, Gene, for his encouragement. There have been many sleepless nights where I have been constantly writing, and you never gave me any grief. I can officially say that I give full credit of writing a book to my daughters, Brittany, Bryana, and Giona

I would like to thank my sister, Alesia, for her understanding and support. I love how you never doubted me. I also want to thank my family and friends for encouraging me to write this book.

Last, but not least, I would like to acknowledge my best friend, Author Vuanu Wood, for showing me how easy it is to self-publish. Thank you.

Author's Message

The emotions and personal experiences that I have gone through in my life inspired this book. There are many women experiencing some of these issues every day, and I just want them to know that they do not have to go from one unhealthy relationship to the next before they find true love. I have many mixed emotions about my life. There are some women that tell me that I should be proud to have had two husbands. These women are not married and have never been married. I, on the other hand, have been married more than once and am currently married. Then, there are others who think the opposite. They wonder how and why I have had so many husbands before age forty. Is there something wrong with me? I always thought that when you get married you are supposed to be in love with that person for life. I never intended to be married three times. Things happen, though. I hope that you can take some of my life's experiences and change something that is not going well in your life. If some of us pay attention, we can avoid going through mentally and physically abusive relationships.

PREFACE

I was born in Riverside New Jersey in 1971. I was raised by a beautiful single-mother. My mother raised four of us: Alesia, James Alfred, James Dennis, and me. Alesia is four years older than me. Then, there was my brother James Alfred, and my other brother, James Dennis, who is one year younger than me. My mom mentioned she was extremely in love with my father. That is why both of my brothers' names are James. One is named after my Grandfather and the other is named after my father. Since both my brothers had the same name, we called my younger brother, Bubbles.

We had a healthy upbringing, with morals and manners that we instill in our children today. Everything was not always peachy keen, but it was not the worst that it could have been, either. My mom was the type of woman who did not want to ask anyone for anything; she would work two and three jobs just to keep food on the table and a roof over our heads. She would even walk when she did not have a car. I know my strength, determination, and ambition come from my mom because there was no stopping her; she did what she had to do to raise her family. My mom would always tell us that *nothing beats a failure but a try*, meaning that if you do not try something, you will never know if it will work out. She also managed to retire at the age of fifty-seven from the Department of Corrections, and now she has started an entirely new career as a Security Guard. I cannot thank my mom enough for being the mom that she was and still is today. Even though my mom was not the type to ask for anything, she received a lot of help from my aunt and uncles and my grandmother, when it came to babysitting us children. We called my grandmother, Ada Mae, Nanny. Nanny will definitely always be in my heart and memory because of the strong woman that she was.

It was a blessing to have my Aunt Ann and Nanny around. My Aunt Ann was a major influence in our lives, and I love her to death. She was like a second mother to us. She would take care of us most often when my mom had to work. Nanny was there right along with her. Aunt Ann had two sons, Ira and Willie. They both are my heart. We are the closest out of all my cousins because we were always together.

Since my father was not around, my Uncle Johnny was the ultimate father figure for us. Whenever my brothers got out of line, he was always there to straighten them out for my mom. I am grateful to have had him be a part of our lives, because I believe every little boy should have a positive male role model in his life. I would rate my Uncle Johnny as being the ultimate husband. One thing that I can say, if there were any problems in his and my Aunt Karen's 's relationship, we never knew about it because everything just seemed perfect. My uncle cooked, cleaned, and he loved his wife. I am happy I was able to witness a marriage like the one that they shared; otherwise, I would think that true love was not possible.

We moved around a lot when I was a child because my mom tried to make it the best way she knew how. We moved from Cinnaminson, to North Philadelphia, to Beverly, to Willingboro, to Florence, to Moorestown, and to Camden. There seems to be a piece of me left in each one of these towns. My best friends were Vuanu from Willingboro, and Janine and Michelle from Florence, in which I have the fondest memories. I made a slew of other friends and associates along the way. Some I will cherish for the rest of my life.

Camden is my last known destination before my adulthood. I attended Woodrow Wilson High, starting at my eighth grade year. In Camden, we lived in a duplex. Alcsia lived in her own apartment downstairs from ours. My sister had her own apartment with three of my nieces: Ericka, Jessica, and Brandy. I considered them my babies because I always had them. My sister always wanted to hang out with her friends, so she needed me to babysit. I did not mind most of the time, unless I had some place to go.

While at Woodrow Wilson, I met my first love, Willie Moore. Willie was so handsome to me. I loved the way he looked at me. He would look at me as if I was the most beautiful girl in the world. I could not resist touching his caramel skin and slim build. He made my heart skip a beat every time I laid eyes on him. Some would not call it love, but Puppy Love. We went through so much together. I loved him, and I just wanted to be with him forever. We got along so well. I loved how he cared for me. He would never disrespect me or mistreat me in any way, and we just understood each other.

I loved the way he called my name because he would always call me Kimberly instead of Kim. He really was the only one that could get away with calling me that. It felt like my mom chastising me, if someone called me by my full name. My mom did not like Troy because he was a young boy and young boys could be influential. What some parents do not understand is that it takes two to tangle, and a boy is not going to do anything that a girl will not allow him to do. My mom was the type that did not want any children in the house when there was not an adult around. We would listen most of the time. Alesia was our babysitter and she would let us have company so that we would not disturb her and her company.

My mom would always tell Troy and me not to get too involved with each other, but the stricter she became; the more we wanted to be together. I was devastated when I got pregnant with his child at 15yrs old. I did not plan on getting pregnant, but when you are sneaking around and not using protection, you can't expect anything different. I felt like I wanted to die when my I missed my period for two months. What was I going to do with a baby at such a young age? All I could think about was how my mom was going to react. I was so young in the mind that I tried drastic measures to try to lose the baby. I punched myself in the belly and even drank this green bitter liquid that was supposed to make you have a miscarriage. Of course, nothing I tried worked, so I had to break down and tell my mom. I mentioned to my mom that I didn't want to have a baby right now. Therefore, I got an abortion. I know it probably was the hardest thing my mom had to do. Immediately after I had the abortion, I got on birth control.

Troy had a difficult time on his end, too. He and his stepfather already had a troubled relationship, so there was no way he was going to tell him I was pregnant. Troy later told me that he regretted us not having the baby because he wanted that bond between us to last forever. Since Troy and his stepfather did not get along, his stepfather kicked him out of the house. Troy had no place to go, so he ended up homeless. Troy decided to go to Atlantic City to live, not knowing where he was going to lay his head or get his next meal. I did not know how he was supposed to take care of himself. I felt sorry for him because he really was a good kid.

I would go to Atlantic City just to visit him and to take him money for food. We would go to the all you can eat buffet, and I would just stare at him while he was eating. I really liked the fact that it was me that he relied on to take care of him. Troy was 18 when his stepfather kicked him out of the house, and he never went back. Over a few months of traveling back and forth, I eventually lost contact with him.

LANCE

Before I got serious with Lance, I dated a couple of guys in high school. I was very particular about dating guys that I went to school with because I didn't like too many people knowing my business. Unintentionally, I dated a couple guys from school named, Fred and Robert . Fred was the Star of the football team and I don't know how or why we started talking. I guess it was because I was on the Pom-Pom squad and he noticed me checking him out. Fred and I hung out a few times, but nothing became of it because he already had a girlfriend.

Robert , on the other hand didn't have a girlfriend and we dated for a while before I met Lance. Whenever I was around Robert it was like "Fire and Desire", we couldn't keep our hands off each other. I was so physically attracted to Robert we would always meet up afterschool and go to his house. Things were much easier because I was good friends with his sister, Shelly . Since, Robert and I didn't have a relationship; we just simply stopped seeing each other.

I also had a few girlfriends that I hung out with named Vanessa, Chaquitta, and Joy. I was sort of the quiet type. I wasn't a popular girl, so I didn't hang out with many crowds. My little group of girls was all I needed. We practically lived at each other's houses. We were like family. Chaquitta's birthday is four days from mine, so we always sent each other a card or called each other on the phone. Chaquitta and I always kept in closer contact than we did with the others because of our birthdays.

Lance and I met during lunch one day. He wasn't really my type because he was a little geeky. However, that didn't deter me because I was too. I used to go with him to his house for lunch nearly every day because he lived around the corner from the school. Lance and I ended up dating until I graduated high school. He graduated one year before me and went into the Navy. He was stationed in California at the time. He even came home to go to my senior prom with me. I didn't know where our relationship was headed, but we were still dating.

I was on birth control when I got pregnant the second time when Lance came home for my prom. I wasn't aware that I could still get pregnant while on birth control pills. I was 19 years old and I had just graduated from Woodrow Wilson High School in 1989. Having an abortion this time wasn't even an option. My mom told me I shouldn't have another abortion because I was out of school..

I was a little upset because I was getting ready to attend Rutgers in Camden that August. I was in total denial because I did not want to believe I was actually pregnant again!. When I finally told everyone, I was about three months pregnant, and that February I told Lance. We tried to figure out what we were going to do about the pregnancy and he mentioned that he was going to take care of his responsibilities, so eventually we agreed to get married. At that time, he was stationed in Mountain View, California, and I was still in Camden. I was worried because I didn't know how I was going to attend college with a baby, but I felt I had to do what I had to do. Getting married felt like the only solution to get out of Camden and see the world, and besides, I didn't have anything to lose. I loved my family dearly, but I was not afraid to venture off. I was always an adventurous type person, and I felt I was very mature for my age. Having helped my sister raise my three nieces, at the time, I felt I had plenty of practice.

Plus, at that age, we always think we know everything anyway, so that made things easier. Lance came home again for the weekend and we had a small ceremony at his house when I was eight months pregnant. Vanessa and Chaquitta were amongst the few people that were there. My sister was my maid of honor and Vanessa and Chaquitta were my bridesmaids. Steven was Lance's best man.

Steven Alexander was a nice handsome guy. Lance and Steven were friends for years prior to me, coming into the picture. Steven and I were attracted to each other, but nothing ever happened between us because of Lance.

My father walked me down the aisle, which, felt a little awkward, because I hadn't talked to my father in years prior to my wedding day. Getting married didn't really scare me, but as I walked down the aisle, I was weeping like a baby. All I could think about was my life ending. I was getting ready to have a baby, and my teenage years were over because I was getting married. If anyone were to ask me if I had any regrets in my life, I would say this was the time.

Do not get me wrong. I cared about Lance but I was not in love with him. If I were not pregnant, I wouldn't have gotten married so young. Everything happened so fast once Lance came home for the weekend, and within that period, we were married. And, within a week, I was packed and relocate in California. We got married May 26, 1990, and I moved with him to California where he was stationed. Lance and I were not in love with each other, but we knew what responsibilities we owed to each other for having a baby. I was looking for bigger and brighter opportunities by going to California. I didn't realize how hard it was going to be at the time. However, I always had the ambition and drive to do whatever I thought was best for me to do.

Things were not all peaches and cream; nineteen years old, fresh out of high school, pregnant, just got married and moved three thousand miles away from home. It was a little scary! I became a mother and didn't really know how to take care of myself. I was still depending on my mom. I was confused. I had my first daughter, Brittany Shale'. By the time I gave birth to her, I was twenty years of age. I had no family there to help me with the pregnancy or labor, and Lance was very young himself, just twenty-one, and he didn't know what to do either. During the pregnancy, we fought like cats and dogs because both of us were young and forced to play house. We both didn't know what to expect out of living together and then having a child. He wanted things his way and I wanted things my way. We were still children, forced out into the cold world alone with very little guidance. As for military pay, we didn't have a whole lot of money; we lived off base so our apartment took most of our cash. We ate Oodles of Noodles for days because we couldn't afford groceries.

I gained 38lbs during my pregnancy with Brittany Shale'. She was the prettiest, yellowish baby I ever saw, so cute and tiny; she fit in the palm of one hand. It is one thing to help raise someone else's kids, but it is a totally different story when those kids are your own. I didn't really know how to raise a baby, but I learned quickly. I literally had to sleep in the opposite room from her because I would wake up at the drop of a dime. She would just be turning over, and I would think that she was waking up.

Since I was away from home, I didn't have a baby shower, but my family pitched in and sent us the biggest box I had ever seen, filled with stuff for Brittany. It felt like Christmas. I was so happy, because I knew we couldn't really afford anything for her. Right after I gave birth to Brittany, within a month I had lost all my baby weight. I was back down to my natural size 7-8 and 138lbs. Then not even a week or so later, I noticed I was picking up weight, again. When I went back for my six- week check-up, the doctor told me I was pregnant again! I was so devastated! I was upset because I was only twenty years old with a baby and pregnant with another. I cried to my mom and she comforted me by telling me that I had nothing to feel ashamed of because I was married.

Lance taught me how to drive when I got to California. Shortly after that, I took the test to get my license. The driving laws are somewhat challenging in California, much different from those in New Jersey. I managed to pass the test after a couple tries, and got my license.

Meanwhile, I asked around on the military base to find a babysitter. One of the military guys' wives decided to babysit while I went to work. I worked at a Target Store in the Snack bar, pregnant with my second child, and all. All together, we stayed in California for about a year and a half, until Lance was relocated to Seattle, Washington.

It was extremely hard taking care of a baby and having one on the way. Lance was always out to sea for months at a time, so I would have to care for Brittany by myself. I was relieved when Lance mentioned that he was going to San Diego to take some classes for about a month. That gave me an out so I could go back to New Jersey to visit my family. While in Jersey, I gave birth to my second baby, Bryana Alise.' By the time she was born, I was twenty-one.. Bryana was a breath of fresh air. She was so cute and feisty with her caramel brown complexion.. She was lifting her head and moving around fast. My Nanny would always say, "You better watch that child, when a baby is progressing that fast, she is moving over for the next baby." I was making sure that wouldn't happen again. I wasn't trying to have another baby, ever!

What was so amazing was once again; I lost all my weight right away. My mother moved back to Moorestown, where she purchased her first home. My grandmother lived with her and my Aunt Ann and Uncle Rick still lived directly across the street, so I was amongst a lot of family. I was glad to be home having the baby because, unlike with Brittany, I didn't have anyone there with me but Lance and he only knew about as much as I did. About a month later, I went back to Seattle. I was a little skeptical about going back to Seattle, but that was my home. It was a struggle having two babies, both in diapers and both on the bottle. I had no transportation there, so I was on and off the bus with a two- seated stroller. It was not easy, especially when the bus came and I had to actually take one baby out the stroller, hand the baby to a total stranger, then reach down to grab the second baby and at the same time close the stroller, and then climb on the bus to take my baby back from the stranger. I had two babies on my lap, trying to balance the stroller so, it wouldn't roll down the aisle. Then I had to repeat the same process to get off the bus. It was humiliating. I felt so alone, but I couldn't go back home, being a married woman with kids. Therefore, I just did what I had to do.

Shortly after, I got back to Seattle, God must have heard my prayers; I received a call from my younger brother, Bubbles. He wanted a change of atmosphere. He came from Jersey to stay with me in Seattle, so that I wouldn't be alone. He had not too long graduated high school. My sister had her own apartment, and my older brother was the last sibling left at home. When Bubbles came up, he helped me out a lot. In addition, I was not feeling lonely. We made friends and would have card games and cook outs. Bubbles was a pleasure to have around most of the time, but then there were times when you had to be serious. I would have to get up to go to work the next morning and

Bubbles would have friends over late at night playing cards or something while the kids and I were asleep. I would be awakened in the middle of the night and go into the living room to find about four or five people in there, playing cards and drinking. I would force them all out. Nevertheless, over all I was happy he was there.

During the time we were in Seattle, I felt neglected in my relationship with Lance. We never had great sex. It was always very quick, no caressing. You would think after two kids and all that things would have been different. I thought I was not attractive enough, as if he really didn't want to touch me. We would have friends over and I would notice that he was super cool with his best friend, Paul. I also noticed a lot of lying about his whereabouts.. Then, one day I noticed a coin lying on the floor; I picked it up and looked at it. The coin belonged to an adult bookstore. I didn't think anything of it.

After about another year and a half, Lance received an honorable discharge from the Navy. He mentioned that he didn't want to be in the military anymore because he kept dislocating his arms and knees. Therefore, the military relieved him without any penalties. We were going back to New Jersey! It was in the winter and the roads were bad. Overall, it took us 7 days and 6 nights to get home. We packed up as much of our stuff as we could in the car along with the girls. It was quite an experience driving back home. The girls were both on the baby bottle and in diapers so they were not that much of a problem during the drive. When we made it back home, we stayed with Mom for a little while until we got our own place on Boyd Street in East Camden.

We lived in Camden for only a few months before Lance decided to hang out in the street with friends all hours of the night. He started drinking heavily and wouldn't listen to me or anybody else. He became very distant. One day Lance stayed out all night and came home the next morning telling me he was packing to go away for the weekend to Washington, D.C. I mentioned to him that he was married and that he couldn't just go away for the weekend. I accused him of being with another female every time he disappeared and he mentioned that it could be a guy. I ignored his comment, thinking he was just being sarcastic. We got into an argument when he decided he wanted to get on the phone with someone, whispering. I went to snatch the phone out the wall and he thought I was trying to snatch the phone out his hand. Therefore, he hit me in the head with the phone. Blood was streaming down my face. He cried saying he didn't mean it and he was sorry. I called my brother James, he came to the house, and said one of us had to leave. Lance said he would leave. He had a few of his friends come to help him move his things out. There were about four, very handsome guys that came to help him, friends that I never saw before. When Lance left, without saying a word to me, I didn't hear anything back from him in about a week. Looking back now, I guess, he must have gone to Washington, D.C. for the week.

The next day I had a talk with Lance's mom, Tamela. She was always there for me when I needed to talk. She was an excellent mother and a fantastic grandmother. That day I told her what happened between her son and me, and I asked her to give me advice about our situation. I had always thought something was going on with Lance, but I couldn't put my finger on it. He was really going through many changes and I thought it was because of us growing up entirely too fast. I asked his mother what was wrong with him. She mentioned that he was what I thought he was. The topic that we were speaking about wasn't the first time, without beating around the bush. Because previously I would talk to her about my insecurities. At that time, I just came right out and asked her if he was gay. I had always had my suspicions, but I was in denial. I didn't want to believe that crap. She confirmed my suspicions and told me her son, my husband, was gay. Mrs. Williams was always close to me. I loved her and her husband as if they were my own parents. She and my own mother always tried to stay out of our business. She never wanted to get involved unless asked. I somehow knew all along that that was what it was. After finding out, all the pieces to the puzzle just seemed to fall into place. The long hours in the bathroom grooming, the baths, his feminine ways, his best friend Paul, the coin that I found, and our awkward intimacy were all signs I should have paid more attention to.

It was sort of a shock to me, finding that out, but also a relief of some kind. I thought there was something wrong with me. I didn't feel good about myself. After I found out that he was gay, I knew nothing was wrong with me. After a few weeks with him being gone from the house, he called to tell me he wanted to come back home. He mentioned that he knew he was gay since he was about 6 years old, and that he was in denial. He would have many girls to take his mind off having feelings of being with a man. I told him I didn't want him back. I was not going to play rush and roulette with my life. After he went out and actually experimented with men, he thought it was cool to come back to me! Since, I was never in love with Lance; it wasn't that difficult for me to let him go. Of course, I felt hurt, because I felt betrayed, but I knew it was for the best. I knew it would have been much easier if he had wanted another woman, because I could compete with a woman, but I could never compete with a man. I just never in a million years could have imagined that my marriage was going to end that way.

Lance and I were young; we didn't really have our acts together. I believe our relationship would have eventually ended anyway. When you get married, it is supposed to be for better or for worse. But, I couldn't stand being with a guy that I knew wanted another man. I remember before getting married, my mom asked me repeatedly, if I was sure this was what I wanted to do. I should have listened to her, but my mom's encouraging words stuck in my mind that, *nothing beats a failure but a try*! How was I to know that my marriage wasn't going to work out? I was just thankful that I had two beautiful daughters as the result of my failed marriage. So all was not lost, I would always be grateful for them, if nothing else.

TYRONE

Lance and I split up February 1994 and Tyrone Jenkins and I met in May of that same year. I was working at Commerce Bank. My friend and co-worker, Paula, asked me to meet her friend's brother. She was dating this guy named, Ray Jenkins. Ray and Tyrone were brothers and they wanted to double date. I told Paula that I was not going out with this guy until I knew what he looked like. I was very shallow and thought looks meant everything. I didn't want to go out with just anybody, so I insisted that I see a picture first.

Paula lived down the street from Tyrone's Aunt Nicole. A few weeks prior to meeting Tyrone, Nicole and I met at a Mary Kay presentation that someone invited me to. We became friends, instantly. Nicole was only a few years older than Tyrone was, and they grew up in the same household as brother and sister. Tyrone's mother was old enough to be Nicole's mother and she practically raised her.

Later that month Paula managed to get a picture of Tyrone, meanwhile I gave her a picture of me to give to Ray to show Tyrone. When I saw the picture of him, I thought he was a very handsome guy, so I told her it would be fine to meet with him. Since it was only a date, I agreed. So one day he came up to the job to take me to lunch. He was just what I liked in a man. He was mature, clean shaved, had a nice physique, good attitude, and was not thug-like. He was the perfect gentleman, and I was impressed.

We started dating. When I met Tyrone, I was on the rebound from having been married, and left to take care of two small children. Brittany was almost three years old and Bryana was almost two years. At the age of twenty-two, I was separated with two small children. I was young and didn't know what I was going to do; I had a mediocre position working as a bank teller. I was barely able to pay my bills, so it was easy for me to latch on to Tyrone the way that I did. I should have known from the door that he was up to no good. We were inseparable for about two weeks straight. I went to his apartment one day to see him, and some girl answered his door. When I tried to talk to Tyrone he up and ran out the house. We didn't know where he went. Therefore, I started talking to the girl and she mentioned that she was his girlfriend. At that point, I didn't want to be caught up in drama, so I began to leave. When I got outside Tyrone came over to my car and told me the girl wasn't his girlfriend. I didn't know what to believe, but from that day forward, we continued to be inseparable. We would stay at each other's houses every night. Within a few weeks of being together, I got pregnant. I knew I was not going to keep the baby because we just met, and I never wanted to have more than one baby daddy, unless I was married. Therefore, I got an abortion. I didn't tell Tyrone about it. I felt it was my body, life, and decision.

Off and on for about nine years, a whirlwind of events occurred. Tyrone was extremely unfaithful to me from the door. Nothing was stable with us. We were very unstable within our relationship and with our home environment. We relocated almost every year since we got together. I didn't want that to happen especially, since I had two small daughters. They couldn't keep friends because every time they met someone we were moving again. Tyrone was in and out of jail for doing stupid things to impress women, like stealing vehicles and motorcycles. He would eat, sleep, and conjure up criminal activity that he could perform the next day. He would cheat on me constantly right under my nose. My family would see him out with other females and he would deny it right to my face. I was so young and naive that I would believe anything he told me, right over my family. He would be so jealous and controlling. He didn't want me going out with anyone but his aunt and then after a while he didn't even like that because Nicole and I became so close. He thought she would lie for me, or slip up and tell me some of the scandalous things he was doing behind my back. At times, she did, but most times, she would keep it to herself because she knew Tyrone and I would get in an argument. I couldn't even go see my family regularly. One time, he disconnected something in my car so it wouldn't start and I couldn't go anywhere.

After a while Tyrone and I would get into fist- fights because neither one of us trusted each other. I knew he was cheating and he assumed I was cheating. I wanted to cheat on him so bad because I was so angry that he was cheating on me, but I was too afraid he would catch me. Tyrone had no respect for women. He thought all women cheated. I believe that is why he felt so comfortable to cheating on me. I really didn't cheat on him. I may have innocently flirted with guys, but I never cheated. The only time I messed with another guy, was when we were not together. I would always feel that if we split up that we wouldn't get back together, so I wouldn't feel guilty about being with someone else. However, we would wind up right back together. For some reason Tyrone always would try to come back as soon as he found out I was seeing someone else. He wanted me to be with him and only him, despite what he would do to me.

One day, unexpectedly, he showed up at my door with a personal pan pizza. I had company at the time and Tyrone said to me, "Tell him to leave, or else I'm going to leave and you won't ever see me again." Of course, the guy left, because he didn't want any problems. Then there was another time that I decided to have a friend over and Tyrone just showed up unannounced and uninvited. He came in and saw that I had someone there and told the guy to get out his house. I couldn't believe he did that because he had moved out a few weeks prior. There was really no getting rid of Tyrone. He always came back. One time he told me I had to leave him because he wasn't going anywhere. I believed him.

Tyrone was just an evil and mean-spirited individual. One day he got so jealous, he told me to get out his car. I was getting out the car, and as I was getting the girls out the back seat, he snatched my wig off my head! All I had on was a wig cap. Thank God, it was about 11pm on a Sunday night and there was barely anyone on the road. Any time we got into an argument, I made sure I took my girls with me. I wouldn't dare leave them with him. I figured if he would hurt me, he might just hurt my daughters, too. But thank God, he never mistreated them, because had he, I would have been gone. I grabbed Brittany and Bryana from the back seat and we began to walk the rest of the way home. As we walked through this long field, I tried my hardest not to let Tyrone see us. I was so stubborn, I wasn't about to get back into his car. Once we made it to the house, he was home waiting for us, to apologize to me. He would always make up with me and then want to have sex.

The sad thing is my daughters witnessed all this nonsense. They would see the physical and mental abuse that went on constantly. Tyrone was five years older than I was so he felt he could control me. I was vulnerable when I met him, so I relied on his every move. Plus, I was deeply in love with this man. I would kiss the ground he walked on. I was so vulnerable that I didn't realize the damage that I was causing my girls. They were unstable, not truly loved by him. Don't get me wrong, Tyrone cared a great deal for the girls, but it's not the same when it is not truly your own biological children. Brit and Yana didn't really know their real father. They were only two and three when I met Tyrone. Bryana was just learning to walk at the time. I know I may have truly damaged my daughters, but by the grace of God, I hope I didn't. We moved so much during the time that we were together. There were so many up and downs that I can't even go into detail how disturbing this was. Tyrone was nothing but trouble and he lived and breathed trouble and irresponsibility.

Shortly after that happened, I stopped working at the bank and went to Business School, to learn computers. I stayed at my mom's house in Moorestown. I was in school for a year, so I could earn a certificate as a Computer Information Specialist. Nanny would watch Brit and Yana while I went to school. Tyrone would come visit me there in the evenings. My grandmom loved Tyrone, she would always say to me, "One day you're gonna marry that boy." Once I finished school instead of going into the computer field, I went into the mortgage industry. I started working for PHH Mortgage Corporation as an Auditor/Post Closer. I liked my position because it paid well, but I had to put in too many hours of overtime. Thank God, my daughters' daycare facility was right across the street. I would sometimes pick them up and take them back to work with me, so I could finish my work. I was always a dedicated and reliable worker. Even though I had children, I still managed to keep a good job. The only area I fell short was with a man. I didn't think I needed a man in my life, but I just wanted Tyrone so much. I was young, dumb, and blinded by his love. When Tyrone and I moved in together, I thought he had his stuff together and he probably thought I had my stuff together. We didn't realize that we were both in the same boat. We didn't have a pot to piss in and a window to throw it out. For the longest time he promised marriage, but I was still married to Lance. At the time, I didn't think it was necessary to get a divorce form Lance because since I wasn't with him anymore, and I didn't have a commitment from Tyrone. Why would I go through all the trouble if I didn't have to? So I thought.

Tyrone was the type that could dish stuff out but was not one that could take it. He felt since he was the man he could do practically what he wanted. His thing was basketball. He had to play ball with his brothers at least two or three days out of the week. I could understand why, he had a great body and wanted to stay in shape. Oh and I can never forget washing his car was a great form of exercise for him, also. He could detail the heck out of a vehicle, making it spotless. For some reason he always wanted me to go watch him play basketball, and he took me with him to get his haircut. I think that was his way of keeping track of where I was or his way of showing me off or something. But, what was funny was how he would get upset if someone tried to talk to me. He knew guys would be around. I just didn't get it.

I would also take Brittany and Bryana with me when we went to the courts so that they could play at the park. I was okay with going because I didn't have anything else to do. Plus, my life was consumed around his and what he wanted me to do. I was his woman and I let him take full control. We would practically live at his brother, Ray's house. We would go over there almost every day. My girls loved it because Ray and Natalie had three children. We had a great time also, playing all sorts of games. There was always something to do over there.

Everything was peachy keen until I didn't do what Tyrone wanted me to do. For example, he wanted me to cook every night. If I didn't feel like it, he would get an attitude. He would cook sometimes too, but when he came home from work, that is what he expected. And, the house had to be spotless. It didn't matter that I worked all day and had to take care of the girls.

Even though Tyrone really wasn't any good for me, I did not allow him to hold me back. I never allowed him or any man to interfere with my education or my career. I knew a man is not guaranteed. He may be here today and gone tomorrow. My primary focus was my daughters, but I still I wanted Tyrone so much. He was like a drug, and I was addicted. For the first time in my life, I realized I was truly addicted to a man. Even though I knew he was not good for me, I still wanted him. , We could both became aroused standing next to each other. We sometimes knew what the other was thinking. We would even finish each other's sentences. There was not anything I wouldn't do for that man.

Tyrone would do some crazy things. We would fight all the time about him going out and I didn't know where he was all day and half the night. He would turn off his pager or cellphone or just wouldn't answer when I called. I would always think something was wrong because I couldn't get in touch with him whenever I needed to. He would always hang out with his brother Barry or Ray and I thought that made me feel better because he was out with them. Come to find out, they were just as bad as he was when it came to females. I didn't trust that any of them to tell me that Tyrone was cheating on me because they were all in it together. What can I say? They were brothers. One thing I can say, Tyrone would give me respect enough to come in at a decent hour.

He would never come in too much past midnight. It was only rarely that he would come in past 1am. In addition, he would always make sure that he cooked and cleaned before he left home. I guess he figured that would make me happy enough to pacify me so I wouldn't ask where he was going. . He would make me assume t he was always going to the basketball court with one of his brothers. I didn't think anything of it because he would tell me to come by at a certain time. Most of the time, I did and he would be there, so that gave me no reason to doubt his whereabouts. Sometimes, I wouldn't stay the entire time, so I am not sure what he did after I left. Sometimes I wouldn't see him for hours after I left him on the courts.

Tyrone had a way of treating me like a lady when he wanted to. He would come to the nail salon with me, sit there, and wait until I was done. I 'm not sure if he was there to look at the other women in the salon or if he was there because he really wanted to be with me.

Tyrone really began to get controlling. He didn't want me to do anything that I wanted to do, especially if he was not a part of it. The only time he didn't care was when he was out doing his dirt. That is the only time I could really be me. Every other time, my moods just adjusted to whatever mood he was in for the day. If he came home upset, it made me upset; if he came home happy, I was happy. It was psychotic. I was not myself. I was so sprung on him I didn't know whether I was coming or going most of the time. One time, my mom came to my rescue because Tyrone and I were fighting. I was so out of my mind that I just didn't care anymore and I was backing into the busy street. My mom grabbed me and shook the heck out of me. She asked me if I was crazy and told me that I could have killed myself. At that point, I knew I was in a self-destructive and unhealthy relationship.

One day I remember calling my ex-mother in law, Tamela. I told her that Tyrone was physically abusive. I will never forget the words that she told me, and those words changed my life forever.

She said, "Do you have a wooden broom, the kind that screw off at the bottom?"

I told her, "Yes."

She said, "The next time he put his hands on you, you go get that broom, and unscrew the bottom. And you wail off on him like there is no tomorrow."

My family gave me advice all the time, concerning my relationship with Tyrone, but their words just went in one ear and right out the other. But, for some reason, what my ex-mother-in-law said to me stuck. Well, I got a chance to act that scene out in little to no time. Tyrone decided to show his behind because I had gotten home late. He wouldn't let me sleep that night. He kept interrogating me until I thought I was going crazy, so I went in the kitchen to get away from him. He followed me, and then he came up behind me, started to choke me and pulled my hair. I was glad the girls were not there that night. I remembered what my mother-in- law told me earlier that evening, and I grabbed the broom. I didn't even have time to unscrew it. I just started to beat the hell out of him I can say now that I really did go crazy at that moment. After that, he apologized to me and we finally had a chance to go to bed. From that night on, Tyrone never did hit me again

Tyrone never hit me again, but he was still up to no good.

One day while I was working at PHH Mortgage, I was going to lunch with my friend Joy Marshall, and I took the wrong turn out of the parking lot. Instead of turning around, something told me to keep going. I spotted Tyrone's truck. I was somewhat shocked because he didn't work there and Tyrone and I were separated. At the time and he was staying with his Aunt Nicole. I had so many problems with him and other women that my heart just sank because I figured this had to have something to do with some other woman. So, Joy and I were trying to find out who was driving his truck. I couldn't even concentrate on my lunch or work when we got back, I was so heated.

I figured the only way for me to find out who was driving the truck was to wait outside and see who got in it. Not too long after I got outside, I noticed a girl get into the truck. I later found out that the girl was someone Tyrone was seeing named, Summer. I knew that Tyrone's vehicles were never legal, and I never understood why he would allow someone to drive one of his cars, knowing they could get pulled over and charged. To be honest, that is exactly what I had hoped would happen to Summer because I was so angry that he was seeing someone else. I didn't concern myself with Summer too long, though, because he didn't treat her right either and their relationship came to an abrupt end.

I started talking to Tyrone again, shortly after that, and he started staying with me again. One day, I used his truck to drive him to work. I assumed that if I were ever stopped by the police, I wouldn't get charged because I had nothing to do with falsifying anything.

Just like, I mentioned before, I was young and dumb. I left his job and about twenty minutes later, a police car pulled up behind me. It was as if trouble followed me. I had a dark cloud over me the entire time I was in the relationship with Tyrone. He mentioned that my registration on the vehicle was suspended. He received my information and noticed that things just didn't measure up. I was given five tickets for various things. I was so upset that I had ever wished this would happen to someone else, and I couldn't believe that it actually ended up happening to me!. I just couldn't believe it!

A couple weeks later, I received a green slip in the mail. The slip mentioned that I had been charged with the possession of a stolen vehicle! I was so devastated. By the time I was supposed to appear in court, Tyrone was locked up again for doing something not showing up to a bail hearing. When I went to court, I told the mediator that the vehicle was not mine and it belonged to Tyrone Jenkins. Tyrone confirmed that my statements were true, and they dismissed my charges.

I was employed at PHH for about 3 years, before I took a higher paid position working for Conti Mortgage Corporation in Warminster, PA. Instead of me commuting back and forth to Pennsylvania, I decided to relocate there. The decision was an easy one for me, at the time, because Tyrone was incarcerated, yet again. The funny thing is, prior to Tyrone going to jail, a pastor told me Tyrone was no good for me. The Pastor actually prophesied to me when I was at a church cookout with Nicole. When we were sitting in the audience, the pastor looked out into the group and asked me to come up to the front. He said he knew something was wrong with me. He asked me if I was having problems with my stomach. I told him that I was. He told the four women around him to place their hands on my stomach. He told me that there was a man in my life that was causing me a lot of anguish and stress. He asked me if I wanted that person out of my life. I told him yes. I knew Tyrone and I had a toxic relationship, but even though I did not want him in my life, I continued to take him back. The Pastor then prayed for me and told me that within two weeks that person would be out of my life. I cried because I was so amazed that the pastor knew what was going on in my life. I also cried because it was confirmation that I really needed to let Tyrone go, but we had gotten so used to each other. The toxic relationship had become a normal way of life for both of us. Within that week, Tyrone and I were getting into it more and more. Finally, I told him he had to leave. He didn't want to go so I went to the police and got a restraining order out on him. I changed the locks on the door and had his bags packed inside the house by the front door. My sister and I went somewhere that night and when we came back to the house, I looked around making sure he didn't get into the house some kind of way. I was afraid of what he might do if he were to get back into the house, so we took precaution by looking around before I got some of my things together. So, when we got into the bedroom I opened the closet door to make sure he wasn't in there. I didn't see anything so I began to get my clothes together, and all of a sudden, Tyrone jumped from the attic portion of the closet! I screamed and started shaking. My sister didn't really care for Tyrone any way and wanted to fight him every chance she got, so that just gave her a reason to dig into that ass. She went after him and tried to fight him and he told her he just wanted to talk to me. I told her it was not worth it. All I wanted to do was get out of there. When I got back to the house, he was gone with his clothes.

About a week or so later Tyrone went to jail for not appearing in court. Bounty hunters came to my house and bum rushed the door when I opened it to see who it was. About ten men came crashing into my house with flashlights, looking around trying to find Tyrone. They were interrogating me with a million questions, asking me where he was. They also checked my car and knew my name and everything. I kept telling them I didn't know where he was, but they kept threatening to take me to jail and put my children into foster care. I was so afraid. I didn't know what to do. However, I did remember telling Tyrone that I was not going down for anything that he was involved in, so once they said that about my daughters, I told them where he was. They went to his aunts' house and picked him up. Whenever someone threatens to hurt my kids, I am like a lion protecting her cubs. I will fight until the end. I didn't want to go to jail behind someone else's stupidity, and what would become of my daughters if something like that happened?

Tyrone was locked up for about nine months for not going to court or something. I thought back to when the pastor prophesied to me at the church cookout. *That had to be a sign that God was giving me a way out of a bad relationship.* Tyrone was incarcerated. I could go on with my life. So I thought….

Within a couple weeks, I went back to him. I felt sorry for him. I relocated to Pennsylvania for work. I worked for CitiMortgage at the time. Every single day for nine months after work I would go pick up Brit and Yana from the after- school program and we would ride all the way to Burlington County Jail to visit Tyrone. We had to talk through a window on a phone. While Tyrone and I would talk, Brit and Yana would be doing their homework. At that time, we made the decision for the girls to start calling him daddy. They were about six and seven at the time. I knew it hindered the girls to have to go to the jail every night, but at the time, I was only thinking about Tyrone. I let my emotions get in the way all the time. I was so addicted to him that I cared more for him than my own children. I thought that going to the jail every night was not going to hurt them as long as I made sure that they had dinner in the car on our way there. They did their homework once they got there and were sleep at a decent time because they would sleep in the car on the way home. By the time they were home, I would just put them to bed for school the next day. I would continue that routine every night and then go to the jail again on Sundays for a visit where we could actually see each other face to face. I felt I was obligated to go see him because he was my man. I always felt sorry for him, not realizing that he put himself through those unnecessary changes, because like I said before, we all have the power to make choices. Tyrone just continued to make the wrong choices repeatedly.

When Tyrone got out about 9 months later, he still had not learned his lesson. He was worse than ever. He got to the point where he was calling females from my house. He just didn't care. When I would answer the phone, they would hang up in my ear. I would see him riding by with other females in his car and find phone numbers that he forgot to take out his pocket. He was a mess.

One day he mentioned that he wanted some speakers for his truck. I was upset because I knew he was up to one of his schemes again. I knew we didn't have any money to buy anything, so he told me to write a check to see if it would go through. I thought to myself, the worst that could happen is the check won't go through and we would be on our merry way. I always wanted to satisfy him, so we went to the radio store. While I was inside the store, trying to pay for the speakers, I didn't know that Tyrone and another guy were putting the large speakers into the truck. Of course, my check wouldn't go through, so I went outside to get into the car. When I got in, I told Tyrone the check didn't go through. As I was saying it, he was already driving off. He failed to mention that the speakers were still in the car. When we were almost home, he told me about the speakers. I told him he had to take them back because they had my name and address from the check. He said he wasn't taking them back and nothing would happen to me. About an hour later, the police came to my house and told me, they were going to arrest me if I didn't take the speakers back to the store. Without any hesitation, I took the speakers back. Meanwhile, the store had already pressed charges against me. Instead of taking care of my business like I was supposed to, by going to court and paying the fine and so forth, I moved and didn't follow up on my mail. I had no idea there was a warrant out for my arrest.

About a year or so passed, I was still following behind Tyrone, digging myself deeper in a hole. I wouldn't listen to my family and friends when they told me Tyrone was no good for me. I thought he was the best thing for me. I loved his family, even though I thought his mother blamed me every time Tyrone got into trouble. No matter what, I gave her the respect that she deserved because she was his mother. I loved the closeness of his family, even though everyone had their difficulties. Tyrone loved his mother, and I didn't care that he was a mommas' boy. We always had family gatherings. He was so controlling that I had begun to know his family more than my own.

Tyrone always used the excuse that he couldn't marry me because I was still married to Lance, so I got a divorce from Lance on April 7, 1999 and married Tyrone on October 23, 1999. My wedding turned out very well, but in less than a year we started having problems again. He got even more controlling. One night he and I had gotten into it and I just wanted to get away from him. One of his family members told him that they saw me out at a club and I was dancing provocatively on another man. Tyrone confronted me about it and I made it clear that it wasn't true. But he didn't believe me.

He was in one of his interrogating moods, again. I called my sister because he was acting crazy, again. My sister and her friend Angel were there in no time. I couldn't believe they drove from Jersey to Pennsylvania in less than 40 minutes. I packed what I could for the girls and me and we left with them. I had already made plans to go to Georgia to stay with Lance, so that I could start a new life in another state, as far away from Tyrone as possible. I knew if I stayed in Jersey there would have been a possibility that we would wind up back together. He knew how to get to me. I figured, if I was nowhere to be found, that wouldn't happen. Before I left New Jersey, I specifically told Lance when I made the plane reservations that I was coming to get away from Tyrone and to start a new life. I made it clear to him that we were not going to get back together, so I thought. I told him that I needed a place to stay until I got on my feet. At the time, I was not aware that Lance had other plans. Once I got to College Park, Georgia, Lance started calling around telling people that his wife and kids came back to him. I had to set him straight and inform him once again that I was only there until I found some place to go. I stayed with him for about a month, meanwhile looking into unemployment and housing. I started attending Creflo Dollar's church, which I was extremely impressed with because I always watched him on television back in Jersey. I met many nice people that attended the church and a selected few knew why I was in Georgia. I thought I was starting to accomplish things when one woman suggested that she had a car for me, I would also spend time with Lance's sister, who lived not too far from him. Before I could even get the car, trouble struck.

Lance and I started to get into arguments because he was upset that I didn't want to sleep in his bedroom. Lance mentioned to me that if he was to ever be with a woman again it was going to be me. He wondered why I slept downstairs with my daughters on the pull out couch. He truly thought that we could pick up life where we left off years prior.

I talked to my family every day in Jersey. Alesia told me Tyrone was at her house every day for a month, begging her to tell him where I was. She never did. So, he asked her if he bought me something for Christmas would she give it to me. She did. He brought me a brown suede coat with a pair of brown boots to match. He also sent me money to buy Brittany and Bryana something for Christmas. I was touched by his gifts because that showed me that he cared. Was it just a tactic to get us to come back home? I don't know. My sister also said he was walking around with a bible every day, telling her he prays everyday asking God to send us back to him. I didn't know what to think. Part of me was saying go back and another part was saying you are away, stay away.

However, everything changed for the worst when Lance told me to take my wedding ring off, still frustrated at the fact that I wouldn't sleep with him. I told him I couldn't do that that I was still married. What I was really saying was that I was still in love with my husband and I wasn't ready to take that step. I didn't believe I would ever get back with Tyrone, but I still loved him. And it was my choice when I decided to take my ring off, not his. We got into a very bad argument and I told him I was leaving. I told him I needed the key to the mailbox so that I could get my unemployment check. He refused to give it to me. I went to grab the key out his hands, and he pushed me. I was going to hit him with a brush that I had in my hands, but he called the police and had me removed from his home. Since I didn't have much to take between the girls and my stuff, I gathered everything and we waited outside until his sister came to pick us up. When his sister got there we waited by the apartment mailboxes until the mail carrier came, and I got my check. I went to her house until my flight came.

Brittany, Bryana, and I were on the plane heading back to New Jersey on New Year's Eve. January 1, 2000, Y2K. That was the year that everything was supposed to shut down; computers were supposed to go hay wire, people's money was going to be lost in their accounts, and planes were supposed to fall out the sky, and that the world was going to end, etc. I wasn't worried though. I prayed before we got onto the plane and I was fine after that. I couldn't get too worried with Brittany and Bryana with me anyway. I had to stay strong for them. When our flight landed, my sister ordered the Rapid Rover to take us to her house. When we got there, everything was nice and quiet for about an hour. Then Tyrone showed up. He wanted to talk. Once again, in a vulnerable position, I went back to him. The girls and I stayed with my sister for a little while until I got my apartment in Moorestown.

Tyrone and I moved there together. He was fine for a little while. We would have little gatherings at our house and play pool and Ping-Pong. Tyrone was always big on football, so he started going out to see Monday night football. They always say when a person changes up his routine there may be something going on. I started to notice that he stopped wearing his wedding band. He would tell me he took it off to wash his car and forgot to put it back on. Also, I noticed his wardrobe changed, and he would get a haircut more frequently. I would notice that he sometimes smelled like perfume. We would argue, but I had no real proof. One day when he was asleep, I went out to his truck to look around. I saw that he had his pager on the sun visor where he normally kept it. I looked at it and it was turned off. I turned the pager on and there was nothing. So, I still wasn't satisfied. I checked the glove compartment, checked in the trunk, and the back seats. Something told me to check under the driver's seat, and to my surprise, there was another pager. I never saw this pager before. It was on, with a single number on it. I went into the house and dialed the number. A female answered the phone. I asked her who she was looking for and she said, "Brian." Tyrone had changed his name to get a job and to work under the table, since he was in the system. I proceeded to tell the female who I was and I asked her what her name was. She told me her name was Moesha. I was so upset that I told her everything about him. She wasn't rude or angry or anything. I thought she understood and that she wouldn't continue to see him anymore. I was wrong. I soon found out that she was younger than I was and she attended Trenton State. Once again, I was devastated. Tyrone woke up and was outside working on his truck when I went out to let him know that I had been talking to Moesha. He looked at me as if he had seen a ghost. I just hit him over the head with the phone. It scattered into pieces on the ground. He came after me telling me that he didn't know what I was talking about. He tried to deny everything and he told me the pager was his brother, Barry's. When I told him everything that the girl told me, he couldn't deny it any longer. He started crying because I told him he had to leave. He was trying to apologize, but I was tired of going through so much with him. I forgave him once again. I wasn't in the position to just up and leave so I made plans to leave the beginning of that year. I waited around until my income tax came. Meanwhile I secretly went and applied to supplemental housing in Cherry Hill, NJ. I explained to the complex that I was a single mother with two children and that I was in an abusive relationship, and I had to get away from him. By that time, we were not physical any more, but the verbal abuse was still there, and he was still seeing another woman. So, the apartment complex approved me. They told me I could move in that following week. That entire week I took mental notes of what I was going to take with me.

The day that I was ready to leave, I saw Tyrone off to work. Meanwhile I had already called my mom and told her that I was getting a U-Haul to move out. Like always, my mom was there. She never questioned my judgment, especially when I made the decision to get out of a bad relationship. Before she got there, I called Tyrone to make sure he was still at work. After that, I packed the truck with all of my daughters' personal belongings and mine. I moved to Sergei Farms that day.

I managed to stay away from Tyrone for a few months. He had no idea I was even in the state. One day I ran into a mutual friend, named Brenda that knew Tyrone's cousin, Monique. That girl went back and told Monique and Monique told Tyrone that the girl saw me at the store. That is how Tyrone knew that I was around and still in the state. I started working a part-time job at a men's clothing store in the Cherry Hill Mall and his brother Barry came in the store to shop. I always did get along with his family. June and I were happy to see each other, but I knew once he left the store, he was going to call Tyrone and tell him. The next day, Tyrone came to the store. Why?

I couldn't believe I fell for him again. He mentioned once again that we were meant to be together. Even though, a few months had passed since I was involved with him, I don't believe that was enough time to get him out of my system. Looking back at the situation, he was probably staying with a family member and wanted to be on his own again. We were back together, and he moved into my apartment. There were always promises that he would do better, and I always tried to have the faith that he would.

However, he would change for a little while and then go right back to being the same ole Tyrone.

I dealt with all this until one day his mischief caught up to me.. Somewhere deep in the back of my mind, I always knew I would be caught up in some mess behind Tyrone. I just did what he wanted me to do. We made a pack that if anything was to happen to me to tell them it was all his doing. He knew that I wasn't about to go down for nothing that he did. I had two daughters to raise, and I was determined that I wasn't going to go out like that. I would write checks for him, believing that nothing would happen to me, or that no one would figure out it was I writing the checks.

Instead of taking care of my business like I was supposed to, by going to court and paying the fine and so forth, I moved and didn't follow up on my mail. I had no idea there was a warrant out for my arrest. That is one of the problems with being in an abusive relationship, you care so much for the other individual that you forget about yourself. You should never be so wrapped up in someone else that you forget about yourself and the people you are responsible for, like your children. If you don't take care of yourself first, there is no way you can properly care for someone else.

One day I had just dropped my daughters off at school. That is one thing that I didn't play with was my daughters and school. I know we have been through a lot, but no matter what or where we were, my daughters rarely missed a day of school. My number one rule was to make sure they did their homework as soon as they came from school. Brittany and Bryana always had fantastic grades, and I intended to keep it that way. I was worried about that at one time because we moved around a lot, but it never caused an interference with their grades. However, this particular day, I was not aware that it would be the last day I would see my daughters for 22 days.

I was on my way to pick up my mother- in- law. I was rushing because I told her I was going to be there by a certain time. I wasn't aware of how fast I was going. At the last minute, I spotted the police officer. The police officer pulled me over for speeding. I was a little upset because I was already in a rush. I knew something was going on with me internally because I was an angry individual. I wasn't myself. I began yelling at the officer wondering why he pulled me over. He ran my information and informed me that there was a warrant out for my arrest. I couldn't for the life of me figure out what it was for. I thought all my business was taken care of. Since I was right in front of the police station, he asked me to pull the car into the lot and to step out the car. At that time, he handcuffed me. I couldn't believe I was in handcuffs, it was so surreal. The police officer led me into the building. I called down the street to Tyrone's mom and sister and told them what happened. They called Tyrone and they all came down to the police station. The police officer told them that I had a warrant from Bucks County. There was no bail or anything until I went to court in Bucks County. I was completely helpless, and there wasn't anything that anyone could do to help me. After going through the paperwork, I was taken to minimum security for 21 days until they could transport me back to Bucks County to go to court. I was so humiliated. I couldn't believe this was happening. I was humiliated and ashamed. This wasn't where I was supposed to be. I cried because I felt helpless, and there was nothing that could be done. All I could think about were my daughters. I didn't know what Tyrone and everybody was going to tell them. All they knew was that mommy would be there to pick them up from school later. I never in a million years thought something like this would happen to me. I cried almost every day in there. I was scared of the unknown. I thought about the horror stories you see and hear on television. I wasn't familiar with the different types of jails. I later discovered there were juvenile, county jails, minimum security, and prisons and more. All I knew was that I wouldn't wish jail on my worst enemy. I also didn't know when I was going home. There was no bail or time for the officers over in Bucks County to come get me. I just had to wait!

Well after crying my heart out the first week, Tyrone finally came to visit me. He mentioned that if I didn't stop crying people would think I was weak and start messing with me. I didn't care. I couldn't stop. I was glad he came, not knowing that would be his last visit, until he came to pick me up.

After, about another week, things started to get better. I started to eat a little bit more. It wasn't as bad as I thought it would be though, I had even managed to make friends. Since it was minimum security, there were no hard criminals in there. There were only people with minor felonies, traffic violations, etc. However, just being in the atmosphere locked away from the world and not knowing when I was getting out was what scared me the most. I told Tyrone to make sure he took care of my daughters and make sure they got to school. We agreed to tell them that I was away on business. That was the hardest thing I ever had to do. I didn't want anyone else having to take on the responsibility of raising my daughters, not even for a day. I arranged for Tyrone to take the girls to school every day and over to my sisters' house on the weekends.

When I was having a hard time, I talked mostly to one girl. She was there because of traffic tickets. Her name was Veronica. She gave me encouragement because she was really into church. Talking to her strengthened my faith. I felt so much better.

Veronica also gave me scriptures to read, while I was alone in my cell.

My sister came once and Nicole and Renee came to visit me. I wasn't expecting my mom to come see me because she was a correction officer. I tried to call her but forgot her phone had a block on it because of her job. My sister also had a block on her phone, so I couldn't even call her. The only person I could or wanted to call was Tyrone. One day I called and the operator said my phone was disconnected. I couldn't believe my ears. I was so upset because I couldn't even get in touch with Tyrone. I felt more and more alone. As the days went on, I became more and more upset. I prayed every night asking God why it had to be me going through this. I started going to this little prayer group with Veronica and some of the other women once a week.

After about the 3rd week of being locked up, you best believe my eyes started to open. I began to get angry. I was furious with myself for allowing a man to dictate my future and turn me into somebody that I didn't want to be. I finally realized I did not need to be with Tyrone. I was given signs after signs, all types of warnings, and I never listened to any of them. God always gives us a warning before the storm. He was constantly throwing signs in my face, and I just couldn't see them. I realized that God had to get me to a place away from everyone, secluded from the world and my familiar surroundings to make me listen. I knew when I got home that I had to do something about this relationship for good. It had to be nobody but God talking to me because I finally opened my eyes. After 21 days, the guard came and got me. He told me that they were transporting me to Bucks County.

I remember there were two police officers that picked me up. They were talking to me on the way to Pennsylvania. The one officer asked, "What is a nice girl like you doing in a place like this?" I told them, "I got caught up in a bad situation." He mentioned that he hoped I learned from this. I told them I definitely have learned from this mistake.

When I got to Bucks County, it was horrible. It looked nothing like innocent, clean Pemberton minimum security. This place looked like the jails you see on television. I was frightened to death. The women even looked scary. If there were woman that liked woman in the other jail, you wouldn't have known, but this one definitely looked like there were some. I was glad the guard placed me in a room that was secluded from the other women in population. She mentioned she did this because I was going to court the next morning. I was so thankful. I stayed in Bucks that night afraid once again for the unknown. I didn't know what to expect. I thought they were going to keep me longer, maybe give me more time that I would have to serve there. It would have taken a lot out of me to go through that. I would have had a hard time surviving that. I went to court the next morning and the judge told me that I had a $428 fine that I didn't pay from about 2 years ago. He asked why it wasn't paid and asked me if I relocated. I told him yes. He asked me how long had I been retained, and I told him for 22 days. He then told me I was free to go. I was so happy I started crying again.

I called for Tyrone to come pick me up. It took him forever to come get me. I was so happy that I was out of jail that I waited for him outside. I didn't want to be in there another minute. When he did pick me up, it felt like I was with my brother or something. I couldn't even look at him. I hated what happened to me because of him. I couldn't believe I had just done time for his foolishness. I realize that I was in the wrong for not handling my business, but If I wasn't associated with him, I wouldn't have been in the predicament in the first place. The entire way home, we barely spoke because there was nothing to say. I simply asked where my daughters were and left it at that.

When we got to my apartment, I couldn't stand the sight of Tyrone, especially, after checking everything out. I was losing my place because the rent wasn't paid. Tyrone took all the money and was doing what he wanted. I found out he had his brothers living in my house the entire time and had their girlfriends in my house. Every single sheet in the house was dirty and shoved in the closet. There was no food in the refrigerator. My cousin, Rhonda lived in the front of the complex, where there was only one way in and one-way out, and she mentioned that she saw Tyrone with a girl in his car. It was just one thing after the other. I couldn't take it, anymore.

About a week went by before I got rid of him. I felt so betrayed, and I was still trying to recoup from being locked up. I had given my car to Tyrone's mom that previous year, down south because Tyrone had two other vehicles. I was using his Pathfinder while he drove his car, so one day when he went to work I packed up the truck with all his stuff. I tried to put as much as I could into the truck. I figured, if there was anything else that he had to get he could come back and get it later. I called my mom once again so that she could follow me to his job. When we got to his job, I parked the truck and went inside to give Tyrone his keys.

When I handed him the keys he asked, "What are these for?"

I then told him, "It's your keys to your truck, and all of your belongings are in it!"

He looked amazed, and started his famous cry. I proceeded to walk away, and I got into my mom's car.

Tyrone went to my mom's side of the car and asked her, "Why is she doing this to me?"

My mom said, "This is her decision." My mom took me back to my apartment, where I had begun to change the locks. It had to be about an hour later when Tyrone came knocking on the door with his brothers to get the rest of his stuff. He was trying to convince me to keep him and make things work. I knew we couldn't go on like that. I didn't trust him at all. Not even a little; he lied for the hell of it. I also would never forget the fact that I had to go to jail, locked away from my daughters for 22 days without them knowing where I was. He only came to visit me once, and I went every single day for 9 months to see his ass! I had never in my life been away from my girls, and I couldn't forgive him for that. I was supposed to be there to protect them and I wasn't. I didn't want to entrust my daughters to anyone else. I felt that was and always will be my responsibility.

So there I was, no car, losing my apartment, and no job. I was a nervous wreck. I knew that things would eventually get better. I just didn't know when. At that particular time in my life, I thought I needed him the most. However, after undergoing what I went through, I knew that I had to do what I had to do. I had to step out on faith; I knew that I couldn't be with Tyrone, though. Women have to realize that when you get to that point when you know enough is enough, you will know. I don't care if you are down and out and think you can't make it, God will always provide a way. You just have to believe.

Within a week, my mom went out and bought a new car, so she gave me her old car. After putting applications in at other mortgage companies, Freedom Mortgage hired me. My mom's friend, Mark, also gave me money to pay my rent.. It just seemed like everything was falling into place. I was not struggling at all. I was fighting with Tyrone almost every night because he kept showing at my door, thinking I would change my mind. I wouldn't let him in because I wasn't ready to talk. I would wind up calling the police until he finally gave up and left.

I managed to keep him away from me.

It took me months, before I could even hold a conversation with Tyrone over the phone. I had to seclude myself from everything and everyone he was associated with. As much as I hated staying away from his family, basically, the only other family my kids knew, I had to do it to maintain my dignity and independence.

I was happy for the first time in my life. I had peace of mind. My sanity means everything to me. I dated and went out with my friends a lot. It was fun!
After about 6mths to a year, I felt comfortable with my decision of not ever getting back with Tyrone, so it was easier for me to talk to him without getting weak.

Tyrone and I became better friends then, than when we were together. I forgave Tyrone because to me forgiveness is hope that the past could've been different. At that point, I could tolerate him being with someone else because I didn't have to worry about him cheating on me. He was much easier to bear.

By being with Tyrone, it taught me a whole lot. I didn't hate him for us not getting along. I am glad I went through what I did, and I have no regrets. The words ring back into my head that, nothing beats a failure but a try! I tried to make my relationship with Tyrone work, knowing that it was extremely toxic.

Now I know that a man is going to do what he wants to do no matter how hard I try to keep our relationship together. I had to come to the realization that what Tyrone did to me wasn't about me at all. He was acting out his own insecurities. I would always think, "Did he really love me?" because if he did, "Why did he cheat on me?" This I could never understand because I was his 'superwoman.' I cooked every night, placing his food on the table, sometimes, before my own children. I made love to him whenever he wanted it, which was practically every night. I treated him the way he wanted me to, with hesitation. I loved him, so I did everything I could to please him. I thought if I treated him well, he would never run to another woman, so when people say the reason why your man is cheating is that he isn't getting it a home…remember that is a damn lie! If a man has it in his heart to cheat, he will cheat, no matter what. Never be so blind that you ignore the signs of a cheating man.

I started to work a part time job with my friend, Sheryl over at Winston's restaurant and bar. I was barely home with working two jobs and my mom was already helping me with Brittany and Bryana, so I gave up my apartment. I couldn't afford to keep paying rent and I was never home. I liked working as a bar maid/waitress at Winston's. , I would work the weekends and get off at 2am. I was making good money because the place was located dead smack in the ghetto, where drug dealers and gold-digging females hung out. I would average about $200 a night. The guys were always generous with their tips, but it was the females that had a problem with tipping. I guess they figured I was competition.

My nights at Winston's' were numbered. By me not being a city girl, I wasn't aware of the fast life. One day I was working my regular shift and one of the other bar maids told me there was a gentleman sitting at the bar that wanted me to get him a drink. Mind you, the rules of the club was that if you are sitting at the bar, the bartender must serve the person. So, I kindly went over to the guy and told him this. He was persistent and told the bartender that he wanted me to serve him. The bartender agreed. So, he told me what he wanted. I told the bartender, and after retrieving the drink, I took it to the guy. He took the drink out of my hands and placed a tip in my hand. He said, "There is something on that bill for you!" I told him, "Thank you," and walked away to continue with my work. Since he mentioned that something was on the bill for me, I glanced down at it when I got a chance. It was a $100 bill with a phone number on it and it read, 'Manson.' I was shocked because I had never seen a tip so large and furthermore, I wanted to know who this guy was that gave it to me. I pulled Sheryl aside and asked her who he was and she told me he was Manson Brice, the owner of the club on Fandango Street. Okay, so I had a little history on him.

Manson continued to come in on the weekends and ask me, to serve him, I would and the tips would remain the same. One day I thought I was supposed, to work, but I wasn't on the schedule, so I decided to eat dinner since I was already there. I ordered the muscles with linguini sauce to take home with me. As I was waiting for my order, Manson walked in.

He came up, sat right next to me, and asked, "Are you working tonight?"

I answered, "No, I am off. I thought I had work tonight, but I don't."

He then said, "How much would you have made tonight if you were working?"

I told him about $200 a night.

He then said, "I will pay you $200 if you stay and have one drink with me."

Are you kidding, I couldn't pass up that offer, and for just keeping him company. I couldn't refuse. Therefore, I stayed for about an hour talking to him. He told me he liked me and would like me to be a host at his club. He told me that he would buy me a completely new wardrobe if I agreed. He told me the only problem that he would have is getting Michael to agree to let me go. By the way, Mason was good friends with Michael. I was thinking to myself that sounds like a very great offer, but did I want to be the one to decide between Michael and Manson. I had to think about that one. I also told him that I was going through a divorce and that I had two daughters. He was impressed by that. After my drink, he decided to walk me out. When we got to my car, he reached in his pocket and pulled out a wad of cash. He handed me $200. He then handed me another $200 and told me it was for my gas home. I couldn't believe he had just done that. I gladly accepted, though. I had no idea what was to be expected from him for weeks to come.

Manson invited my sister and me out to Karaoke Wednesdays at his club. Alesia and I would go and she would put in to sing, but not me. I can't sing a lick. As soon as Manson would spot us, he would come over and say hello. He would tell my sister that he was going to marry me one day. I would take it as a compliment, but we all knew it was impossible, me being at least thirty + years his minor. Then he would make sure I didn't leave without him placing $400 in my hand and a bag of food for the girls from his restaurant. Man, I thought, I could really get used to this. I was getting used to it when Reese, one of my friends that I was seeing on the side from Champagne's wanted to talk to me.

He said, "Oh, so I see you one of Manson's girls, now!"

I said, "One of Manson's girls, what do you mean by that?" He proceeded to tell me what he was noticing and that Manson was famous for recruiting girls that would fall for being one of his girls that he could wine and dine and eventually sleep with. Whoa, that was all she wrote. Alesia and I stopped going to Manson's club and I eventually stopped working at Winston's. I see how young girls, can get caught up. It is extremely easy when you have someone throwing money at you. However, I was never into that fast, street life and I can't be bought. I was also starting to go to church every Sunday, and I was starting to feel a little convicted, serving drinks on Saturday nights and then attending church on Sunday morning. It just didn't feel right. So I quit!

After a long while, I was dating and I had friends. However, there was one guy that I really started to feel. I met Brendan while working for the mortgage company. He and I hit it off very well. Our personalities clicked, but our relationship didn't last too long because Brendan was into drugs. We had so much fun together, prior to me finding out. He just had a great spirit about him. It is a great feeling when you could be yourself around someone and not have to hide the real you. You don't have to put on any airs. We would sing together, and I knew I couldn't sing. We would go out and just have a good time together. He was the type of guy that had to look good whenever he stepped out of the house. He put you in the mind of Baby Face. I loved the way he carried himself. We worked together selling mortgages and he knew his stuff. He made some money. I liked the fact that he was an intelligent guy. He treated my girls very well, maybe because he had three children of his own. We all would go places together, my girls and his kids. He had two girls and a son. We would go to picnics and swimming, dinner, Dave and Buster, out to dinner, and The Falls. Everything was working out just fine. I just knew we were going to have a future together, until one dreadful night. The phone awakened me. It was about 2am. On the other end was Brendan's mother. She mentioned that she couldn't find Brendan and asked me if I could come and look for him with her. I found this to be rather strange. I thought, What the hell did I get myself into this time? I liked his mom a lot and I knew she was upset. His mother loved her son. That was her baby, no matter how old he got. When she called and mentioned that she needed me to help her find him, I didn't understand. I didn't want to disappoint her, so I went over there. When I got there, she told me that Brendan was on drugs. I couldn't believe it. I thought our relationship was too good to be true.

We drove around to some places that his mother thought he would be, but we had no success. As we were heading back to his mother's home, we spotted him walking. He was so out of it when we picked him up, glassy-eyed and all. He was so ashamed to see me that he just dropped his head. I know he was probably mad at his mother for having told me his secret I dropped them both off at home.

The next morning, I had to make a serious decision if I wanted to continue on this road with him or if I wanted to get out of this relationship. We had a long talk and I told to him that I didn't want to be involved with someone who did drugs. He told me he understood. We parted ways.

MORRIS

Then one day I was at Rent-A-Center paying my furniture bill and met this man named, Morris. This was my first time seeing him. He came from another location. He was very professional, unlike the other guys who always hit on me. I just knew I would be able to go in there, pay for what I wanted and then leave. Morris was so arrogant I knew I couldn't get over on him by paying less on my bill I loved when I met guys like him. It was a challenge for me to see if I could get him to like me and give me what I wanted. He was giving me a hard time because he wanted me to pay the full amount. My brother had just given me money and I didn't want to use all of it to pay the bill. He told me I was late and had to pay the extra fees. I really wanted to hold on to my money because I was going out that night. Plus, the next morning was Good Friday, and I wanted to go shopping with my sister and her husband. Morris and I came to an agreement; he didn't need the full amount at that time. However, before I left, I was checking him out. I thought he was a nice looking guy. I took a mental note of his name. When I left the store, I called the store right back and asked for "Morris." I was in a free-spirited mood, so at that time, I pretty much dated who I wanted to date. I asked him if he was seeing someone, and he said he wasn't. Therefore, I invited him out. We went to dinner at Fridays. I liked him, but he was real arrogant and cocky. He acted like he wasn't that into me. I didn't care, though, I just wanted to see what he was about. We wind up going out again, and things didn't get any better..

My friend, Dorothy didn't like him because he didn't have a car. She knew I didn't like dating guys that didn't have transportation. I worked with Dorothy at Freedom Mortgage, and she had become to be a long-time friend. She was always one to look out for my best interests when it came to guys. Dorothy knew my likes and dislikes when it came to men, so she was unsure about me being with Morris. After I told her he did have his own place, which took precedent over him not having a car, she let up on her feelings about me seeing him I later found out that he didn't have a car because it was recently totaled in an accident.

I liked Morris because he had potential. He was smart and ambitious and kept a steady job. He was intelligent, nice looking, and had respect for me regardless of the circumstances. He was romantic also. I don't know what got into me, but I introduced him to my mother and my daughters. This is something that I never did. I wouldn't let my guy friends meet my daughters unless I knew I was going to be with them for a while. I liked Morris a lot and I felt extremely comfortable with him. We began spending a whole lot of time together, despite how my friends felt about it.

Morris was thoughtful and he made my heart race every time I thought about him. I loved to make him smile, also. One day, right before Valentine's Day, I gathered some candy, a pair of lipstick boxers, massage cream, a couple of adult videos, a couple of adult magazines, and a bottle of cologne. I placed everything in a basket with balloons, had a random lady knock on the store doors after hours, and hand him the basket. I watched from the outside window as he read the card. I could see him smiling from ear to ear. Then all of a sudden, I see him and his co-workers ripping through the basket. They were like wild animals. I knew that was a great gift to give him. The next day I receive a card from Morris that read, 'expect the unexpected.' I didn't know what that was about. Therefore, I kept on with my regular workday. All of a sudden, I received a phone call from the receptionist, giggling telling me that I had something at the front desk waiting for me. When I got to her desk, I couldn't believe my eyes. There was this big gigantic basket filled with fruit and candy. The basket was so large that it took two of us to carry it. It also had three balloons floating in the air that was attached to it. I managed to get it to my desk where everyone started helping me eat the fruit. I never forgot that Valentine's Day. I fell in love with him because he was so thoughtful. He would go out of his way to please me. I felt like a queen. He treated me well and respected my daughters. I didn't want to fall in love again. I wasn't looking for it. I just wanted to continue dating and try to find myself. I found myself spending a lot of time with him. I was at his home when I received a phone call that my Uncle Junior was in the hospital and didn't have long to live. Wow, that was extremely hard because I loved my Uncle. I left Morris to go to the hospital. I had just made it to the hospital before he shut his eyes. That was so sad because all I could think about was my cousins Tim and Brian. My uncle raised them all alone since they were babies after he and his wife split up. It was if they were left, all alone to care for themselves. Since they lived in Atlantic City and we live so far away, they remained there with a guy that was friends with my uncle.

I had another test of faith when I first met Morris. I already had a previous trip planned to go to Vegas with a couple friends of mine. Germaine and Melany worked together and had a business meeting there. Germaine invited me to come along because we were all friends. I met Germaine because he was the director of a children's drill team that both my daughters and their cousins attended. Melany was the instructor that taught the girls how to step. My daughters were a part of the group for a couple years. I had to break the news to Morris, telling him that I will be back in a week. I didn't want to leave him because I was really starting to like him. He also asked me who I was going with. I explained to him who I was going with, letting him know that they were just friends. Germaine was an older man that I liked as a friend. He may have liked me more, but I tried to stay strictly friends with him. I don't recall ever giving him the wrong impression. Later, I found out by a mutual friend that he went behind my back and told her we had something going on. I didn't appreciate him doing that because I never liked him like that. Overall, our time in Vegas was really, fun and I appreciated having had the opportunity to go.

I miss Morris, though. He and I talked every day. When I got back, I was persistent on meeting Morris's mom, but he told me that I might not feel comfortable meeting his family. He mentioned that his mother was always around his younger sister. His younger sister was her favorite. I know what type of person that I am, and I don't mind if someone doesn't like me. I wasn't there for them, I was there for him. When I met his mother and sister, I felt comfortable in front of them. I gave them the respect that they deserved because they were his family. Later, he mentioned to me that his sister said I needed him because I was looking for a father figure for my daughters. She also said I wanted him for his money. I had to address the situation because I never looked for anyone to take care of my daughters, but myself. And, as far as money was concerned, I was never hurting for money. I was making a lot of money working as a loan officer. I didn't need help from anyone. Financially, I was in the best place I had ever been in my life. I was somewhat hurt by that statement, but I got over it, and still respected them. I couldn't take anything they said too seriously because they were a wild bunch who would fight anyone in a heartbeat. They also had mouths like sailors. But regardless of how I felt about his family, I fell in love with Morris. He was a good man.

He was definitely different from the other men I had dated and I was tired of going after the bad boy image. Morris would go out of his way to please me. If my head ached, he would rub it for me. If my back needed to be scratched, he would scratch it for me. He would rub my hairline every night just to make me fall to sleep. He would also kiss my lips and my forehead every day that he left for work. He treated me nicely and most importantly, he respected my daughters. I also knew he was a great provider. He was a good man, and I wasn't going to let him get away. Even though we both had our own places, we'd be at my place almost every night. Therefore, we agreed to move in together. Months after we moved in together, I found out I was pregnant. At first, I was a little leery because my older daughters were 11 and 12 at the time. I didn't know what I would do with a baby 13 years later. Then I thought, I am in love with this man, and I had never been treated so well by any other man in my past. It wasn't a difficult decision to make. I decided to raise a child with him.

I was pregnant for about 3 months, when I started having problems. I was sitting in the movie theater. I felt a little cramping, so I figured I had to go to the bathroom. Since the movie had just ended, I decided to wait to go to the bathroom when we got home. When we got home, I sat on the toilet and noticed there was blood in my panties. I didn't think it was anything drastic, so I didn't want to go to the hospital or anything. However, Morris, after discussing it with his friend, Tom, wanted to call. We went to the hospital and lo and behold, the doctor told me I was having a miscarriage. I had mixed feelings about having a miscarriage. I thought maybe it wasn't meant for me to have a baby. I also thought I might not be able to have any more children. I didn't know what to make of the situation.. Morris was so upset because it was his first child. He felt as if he was being punished or something. He hung in there with me, though, treating me with such good care. Within a month later, I was pregnant, yet again. When I found out, I was so happy. I took precaution with everything I did so that I wouldn't have another miscarriage. I went full term with this baby. It seemed as if the baby didn't want to come out. I mean I tried everything to have her. Brit and Yana would walk a lot with me, hoping that would force me into labor. However, nothing worked. I had two false labors. We went to the hospital twice and they just turned us away. I figured I just wasn't cut out to have a baby because I was 33 years old. I couldn't sleep because it hurt to lay back. I was big as a house. I gained 70lbs. My feet grew two shoe sizes. I was just so miserable, but Morris treated me so well throughout all of it. I had never had anyone show me as much love as Morris did.

The last time I went to the hospital, my mom told the nurse that I was in a lot of pain and she wasn't taking me back home. My mom made it clear to the nurse that I had to have the baby that night. Morris stayed with me that night, and mommy took Brit and Yana back home with her. Meanwhile, the nurse induced my labor and told me to just sleep until it was time.

Morris watched television in the chair by my bed. He was so excited because I was finally getting ready to have the baby. Tatiana Lee was born! My mom walked in with Brittany and Bryana shortly after. Tatiana was beautiful, with a head full of hair. I was relieved because she was out. That was definitely my worst pregnancy. I was even happier knowing I had given Morris a child. This was his first baby, and I could see the admiration in his eyes when he looked at her. I loved watching him with her. I was so grateful to have him in our lives.

I got a divorce from Tyrone in June 22, 2004. I didn't want to repeat the Lance situation, being married while living separate lives. I wanted to be in this relationship with no strings attached. I never wanted to get married again, and Morris never pressured me. However, a couple times he told me that he couldn't marry me if he wanted to because I was still married to Tyrone. I decided to do the right thing. I decided to do my own divorce this time. I wasn't about to pay an attorney, again, for something I could do myself. I got the divorce papers from the Divorce Center and filled them out for a minimal fee. Tyrone was served his divorce papers in jail. My divorce was non-contested, so if he didn't respond within 30 days, the divorce was automatically enforced. Tyrone signed without hesitation.

Morris and I got married February 24, 2007 at the Justice of the Peace in Riverside, NJ. Even though another wedding was not in the plans, I wanted to set a good example for my daughters. I didn't want to be shacking up, and I knew Morris and I were going to stay together. Therefore, we decided to get married at the Justice of the Peace. I didn't want to have another wedding, especially after I had two previous ones. I felt a little embarrassed, as well as ashamed. I just wanted us to get married and get on with our life. We invited immediate family and close friends to a reception dinner with us at Adelphia's. Morris and I have now been married for several years, and I look forward to several more.

EPILOGUE

I should have broken or gone crazy a long time ago, but I have a strong foundation. My mom is a survivor. She raised four children on her own. We didn't have it easy, wearing hand me downs and not even having money extra money to do the things that we wanted to do. She had to work a lot while when we were growing up, just to keep a roof over our heads and food in our mouths. My mom did an excellent job under the circumstances. Not everything may have been done perfectly, but she never gave up. She always told us that nothing beats a failure but a try. She didn't finish high school so there definitely wasn't any college. I realize now that she had to work two and three jobs at a time to support us. One job probably didn't pay her enough to do anything. Just trying to keep a roof over our heads probably was the hardest thing for a single mother of four to do. We had a car some of the time, but the majority of the time, we either caught the bus or walked. My sisters and I ended up doing a lot of things we were not supposed to do because my older sister watched us when my mother wasn't around. My sister wasn't much of a baby sitter because she was doing her own thing. My sister had four daughters of her own. However, one thing I can say is that my mother never had to worry about any of us getting into major trouble like a lot of other children. The worst thing we did was have friends over when we weren't supposed to, and we sometimes went places without permission and so forth, innocent things. We would always have to have the house spotless by the time my mom came home also or else we would get into trouble.

I try to instill in my daughters that we create our own futures. We always have a choice. If my mother would have done well in school and had gone to college, she would have had a good-paying job. Our lives would have been different because she wouldn't have had to struggle so much while taking care of us. I tell my children to work smarter, not harder. By the grace of God, my mother was able to go to the corrections academy and become a successful Corrections officer. She retired from that position at the young age of 56. She is set for life now, with a pension and great medical coverage. She returned to work as a security guard, but she only did that so she would not be bored in her retirement.

I thank God for the experiences I have gone through because they made me who I am today. I walk with my head up high every day. I am no longer going to let anyone steal my Joy. If someone is going to have a negative attitude, I don't want to be around him or her. I will distance myself for a minute or for an eternity if I have to. I can't afford to allow myself to be subject to any negativity. I like knowing that I am responsible for my own happiness. My mind is sound, and I am living a wholesome life. I feel like I can conquer the world. I want to encourage others and let them know that they don't have to be a victim to anything or anyone. You have the power to create your own destiny. Whatever you choose in life, you can achieve. I am living proof. I have never let any of my past interfere with the way I am today. I am always smiling, and I always look good. No one knows my situation unless I tell them or they happen to read this book. I am 40yrs old, and I am in a beautiful relationship. We bought a house and the girls have been in the same school district for 8 years. They have both graduated and have attended some college. They also have a steady group of friends that they actually got close to because they have not been all over the place. It feels so good to have accomplished this for them.

I've been self-employed for a couple years now as a distributor for Ardyss International. I am doing quite well in the business. I love what I do because I am giving back to women to make them look and feel better in their clothes, increasing their self-esteem.

I also founded an organization where I donate prom dresses to underprivileged teenage girls. It all started when my daughters wanted to discard their expensive dresses. Annually, we have a luncheon where we give dresses away to teen girls for Prom. I feel so grateful when I see the smiles on the girls' faces once they receive a gown. I have been receiving donations for dresses and shoes from the community and people around the world, so everyone is helping out.

I also have been making hand-made custom jewelry. I am so grateful that Janie has shown me how to make jewelry. We started out doing it so we could make enough money to pay for office space outside the home, then we decided to make jewelry on a regular basis. I really enjoy putting colors together and experimenting with the different designs. We have been booking shows, and we sell jewelry to friends and family. I love it!

Both my eldest daughters are pregnant, so I am going to be a grandmother twice in the same year. My grandbabies will be three months apart. I still can't believe it. I am so excited, and I am glad they waited until they were twenty and twenty-one before they decided to have children. I am a young enough grandmother as it is.

I just wanted my daughters to complete school before they started having babies.

I'd rather them get it out of the way while they are young because I don't want them to be like me; I only have eighteen credits to get my Bachelors. However, even though I haven't completed college, I have had some pretty well off positions.

It was just the negligence on my part to provide properly over the years and take care of my responsibilities. I allowed others to dictate what I did with my money. I spent unnecessarily, moved often, and wasted a whole lot of money and time. My twenties are gone, and I will never get them back. However, I can say, I have learned a lot from them. I can't put the blame on anyone else. I was the one who could have controlled the situation, but I was young and dumb. On the other hand, my mother was in an abusive relationship and she left my father. However, she had to work more than one job to survive. We moved a lot and didn't develop lasting friendships. There was just not enough stability in our lives. I don't hate my mother for what we went through. I have no regrets; I just know during that time, it was hard on all of us. I probably can't say that for my daughters. I have heard them speak of not having best friends and moving so much. I don't want my daughters regretting what we went through, even though I know they do. However, one thing I can say, the girls have never gone without. They had nice clothes; they had food and a roof over their heads. For Christmas, I always managed to get the girls something, mostly clothes and things that they need. Sometimes I would get some toys. I would always make the girls pray over their gifts before they opened them because I know it was by the Grace of God that I was able to get anything. Now I'm in thirties, and I am so glad that I can finally say I have accomplished some things because nothing beats a failure but a try!

ABOUT THE AUTHOR:

Kimberly Ross was born in Riverside, NJ. She currently resides in Lindenwold, NJ. where she is starting on her second book. She wants people to see that the life that you have lived cannot dictate your future. You do not have to live in bondage. She is living proof. www.kimrosshollingsworth.com

Kimberly Ross is a feisty, gorgeous, smart, and perceptive woman. She is a loving mother of three daughters. She is currently with her husband for over 10 yrs.

Kimberly Ross lives in Lindenwold, NJ, and she is currently founder of The Positively Dressed Organization (www.positivelydressed.blogspot.com). She also has her own hand-made jewelry line called 'Elegant Jewelz'and she is a distributor for Ardyss International (www.ardyslife.com/kimberlyross) . She is currently working on her next book.

Visit us online at www.nothingbeatsafailurebutatry.com

Or email me at kimross6615@yahoo.com.

NOTHING BEATS A FAILURE BUT A TRY KIMBERLY M. ROSS

Kimberly has led a pretty, rough life, when it comes to relationships. Love, loss, and trust have played a major part in her life. From having a husband that was living on the Down Low to having a husband with an ongoing criminal history, now she may have found true love. She had begun to give up and just concentrate on herself!

Her constant struggle with men has led her to her third marriage by the age of 40yrs. She is an over achiever in all areas business, work, education, and socially, but she just can't get it right in the relationship department. Until…

http://www.lulu.com/content/e-book/nothing-beats-a-failure-but-a-try/13064143

www.ingramcontent.com/pod-product-compliance
Ingram Content Group UK Ltd.
Pitfield, Milton Keynes, MK11 3LW, UK
UKHW041918190726
13854UKWH00003B/1303